# THIS BOOK BELONGS TO:

. . . . . . . . . . . . . . . . . . . . . . . . . . . . . . . . . . . . . . . . . . . . . . .

**Silver Dolphin Books**
An imprint of the Baker & Taylor Publishing Group
10350 Barnes Canyon Road, San Diego, CA 92121
www.silverdolphinbooks.com

Copyright © 2009 Mango Jeunesse

Written by Emmanuelle Teyras

ISBN-13: 978-1-60710-338-7
ISBN-10: 1-60710-338-9

Manufactured, printed, and assembled in Dongguan, Guangdong, China.
1 2 3 4 5 15 14 13 12 11

These two chefs each have an apprentice. Draw them so they can all get to work.

**What did these foods look like before they were eaten?
Can you re-create them?**

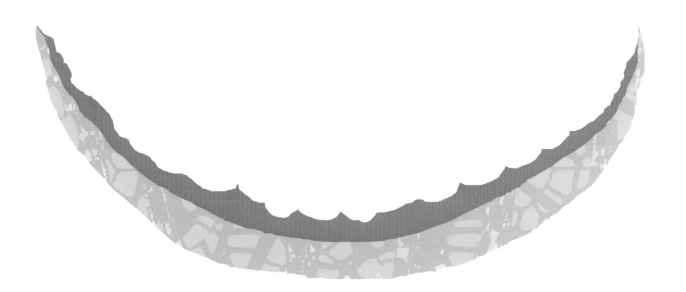

**To complete these pages, draw foods in each box that match the colors.**

**Help the baker finish the cupcakes. Use the colors on the right to guide you.**

**Use stickers to dress the two friends. See the models on the back flap of the cover for some ideas.**

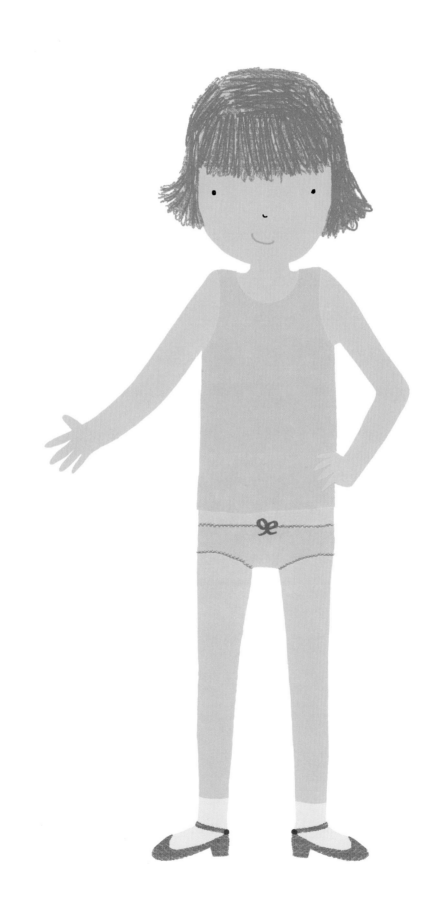

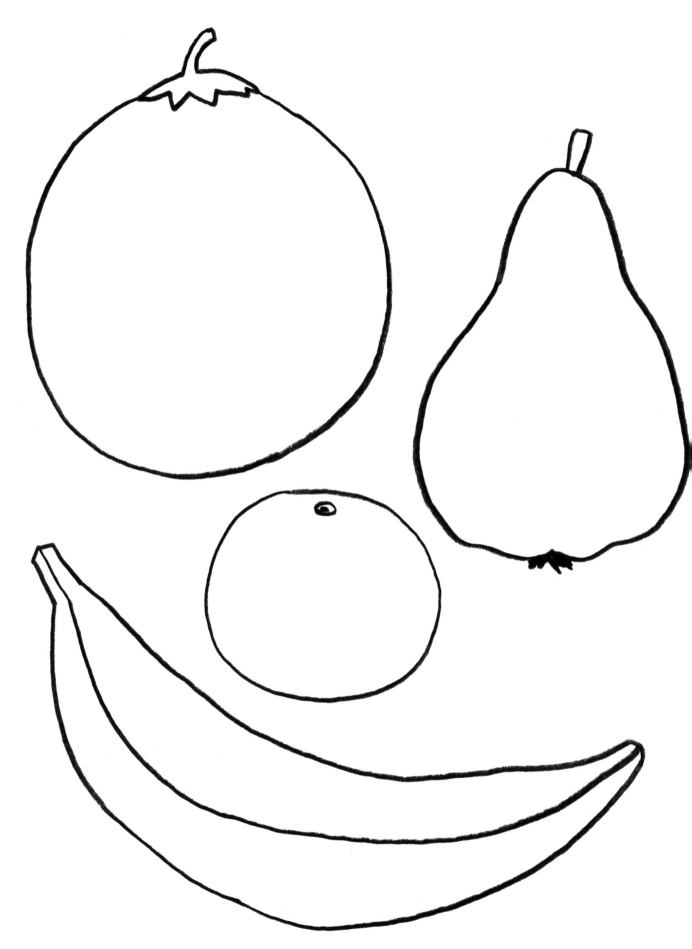

**Color the fruit to make it look delicious.**

# What fruits did you use to make these jams?

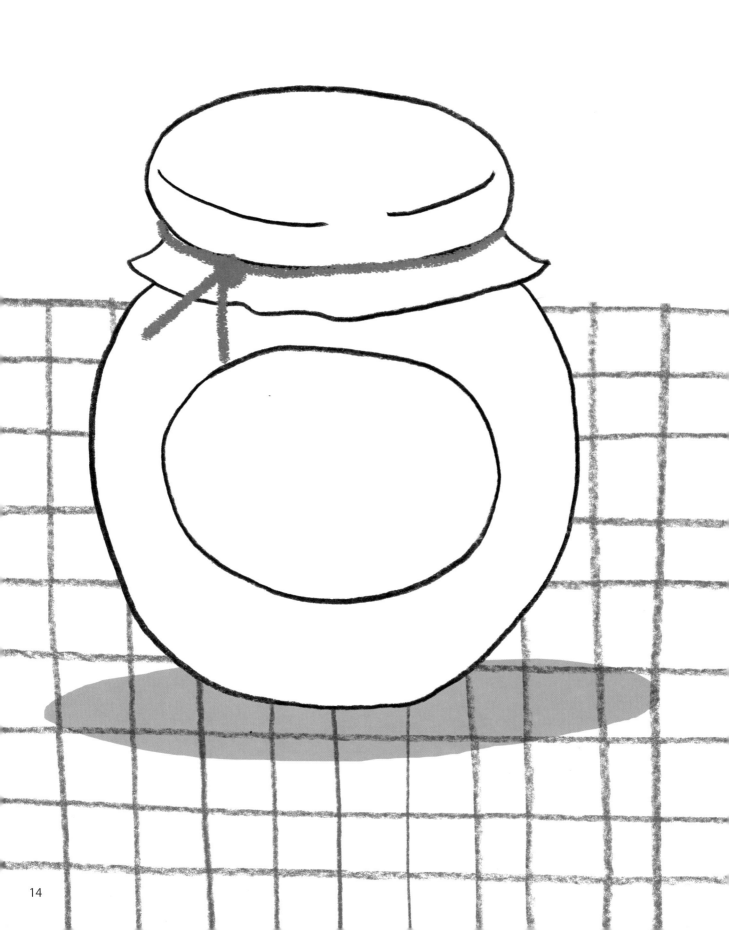

**Color and decorate the jars and labels.**

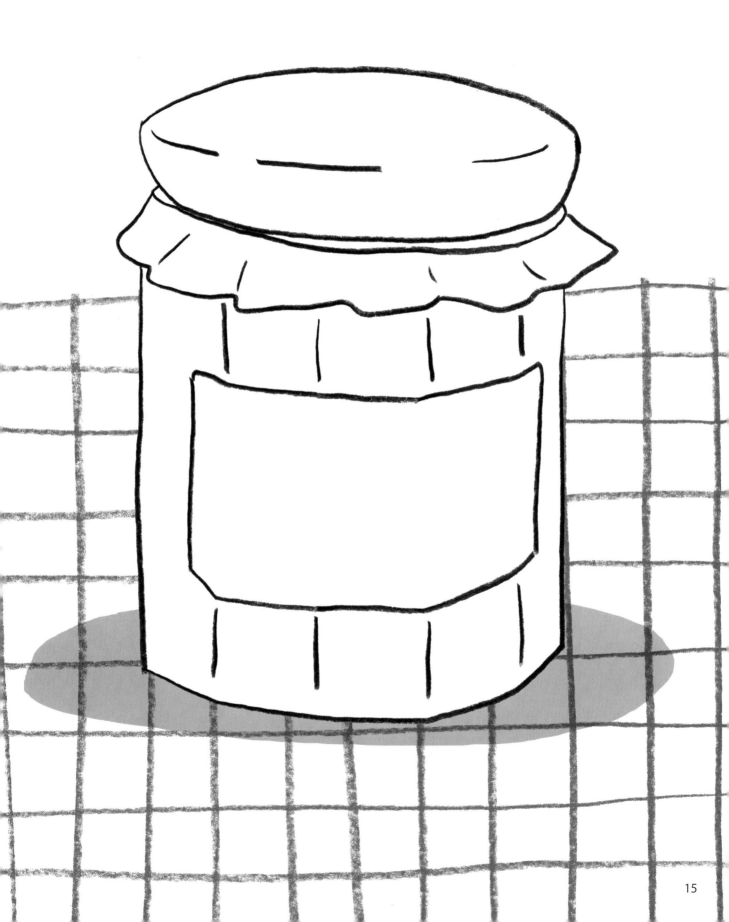

**Cut out the shortbread cookies from the pages at the back of the book and glue them onto the plate.**

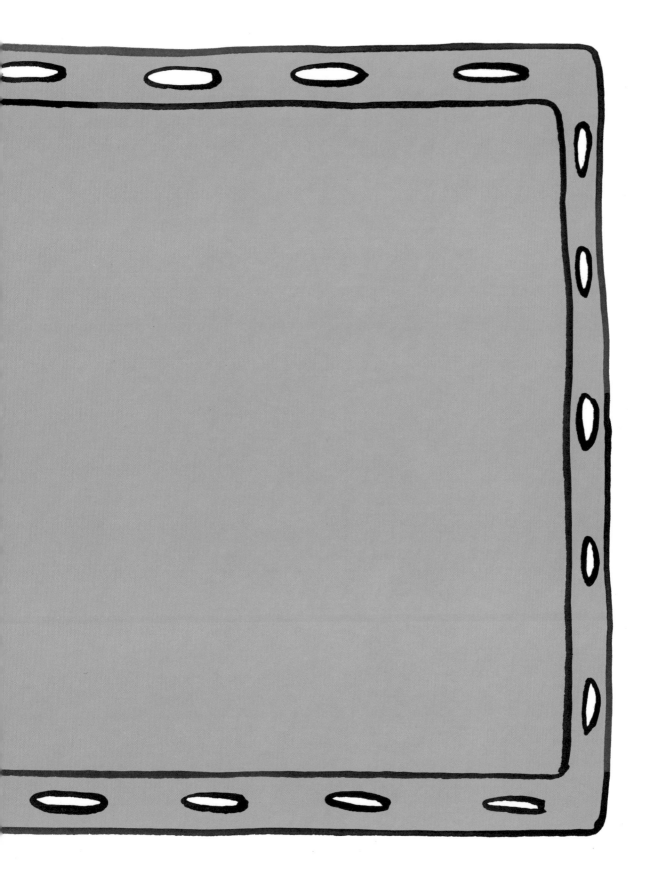

To decorate this page, you need a lot of red! Use different tools:
colored pencils, pens, chalk, and more!

# F f

# A a

# T t

# S s

**Complete this page by drawing items from your kitchen that begin with each letter.**

# O o

# B b

# C c

# P p

**Draw your favorite meal and dessert. Don't forget to decorate the plates.**

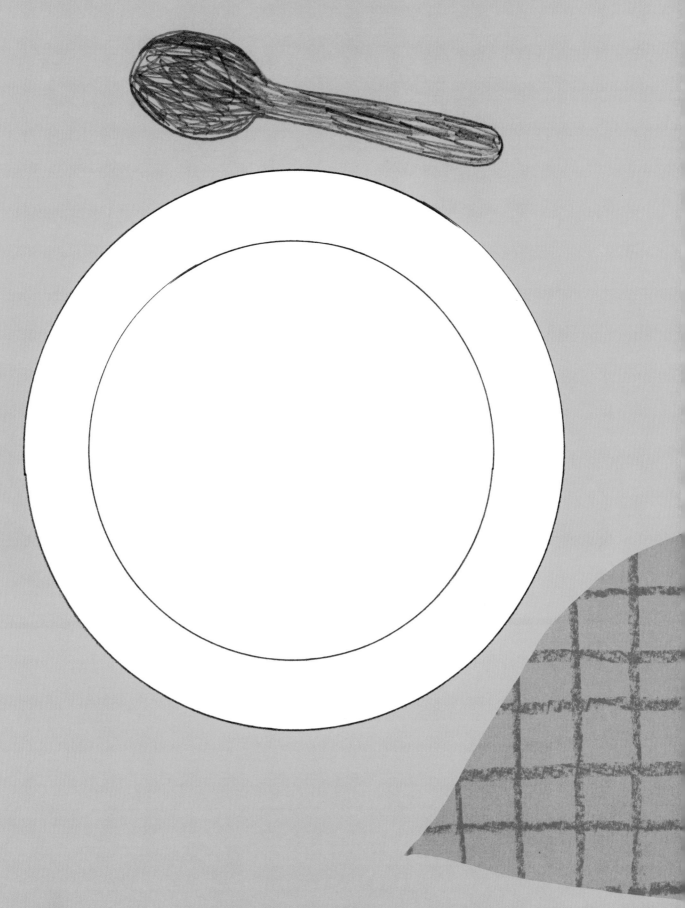

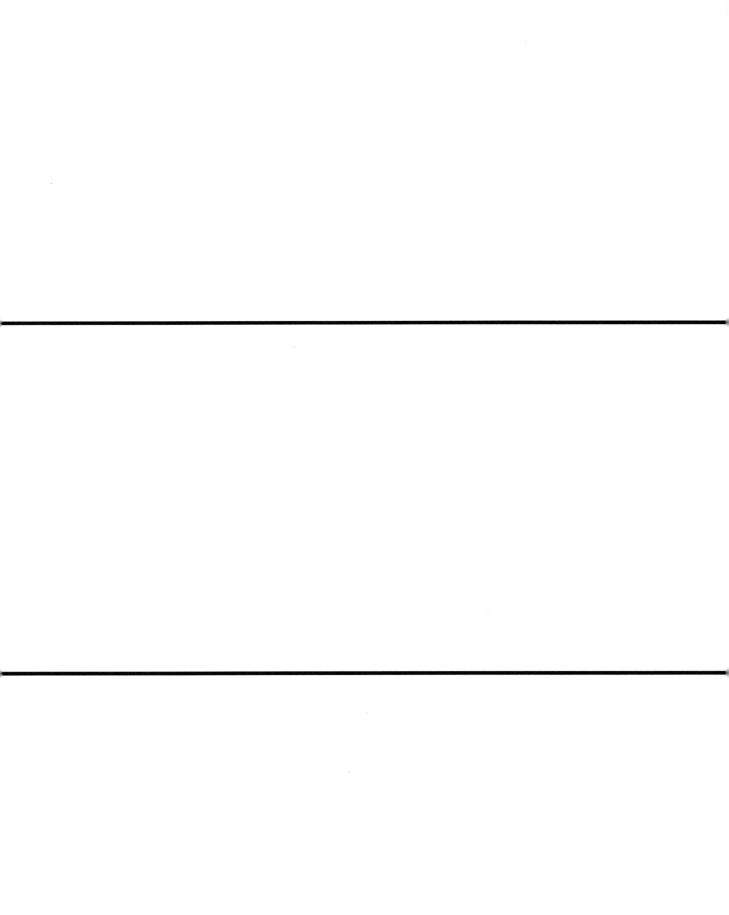

**Write your name in letters that match each pattern.**

**Use the paper cutouts at the back of the book to create a beautiful cake.**

**See the model on the back flap of the cover for some ideas.**

**Fill each jar with the right ingredient.**

raspberry cakes

mini sausages

lemon slices

**Finish decorating the bowls and then fill them with the right ingredients using the paper cutouts at the back of the book.**

eggs

tomatoes

French fries

**Color everything in the kitchen.**

sugar    flour

mixer

**Mr. Pineapple asked Ms. Melon to marry him! Draw their portraits.**

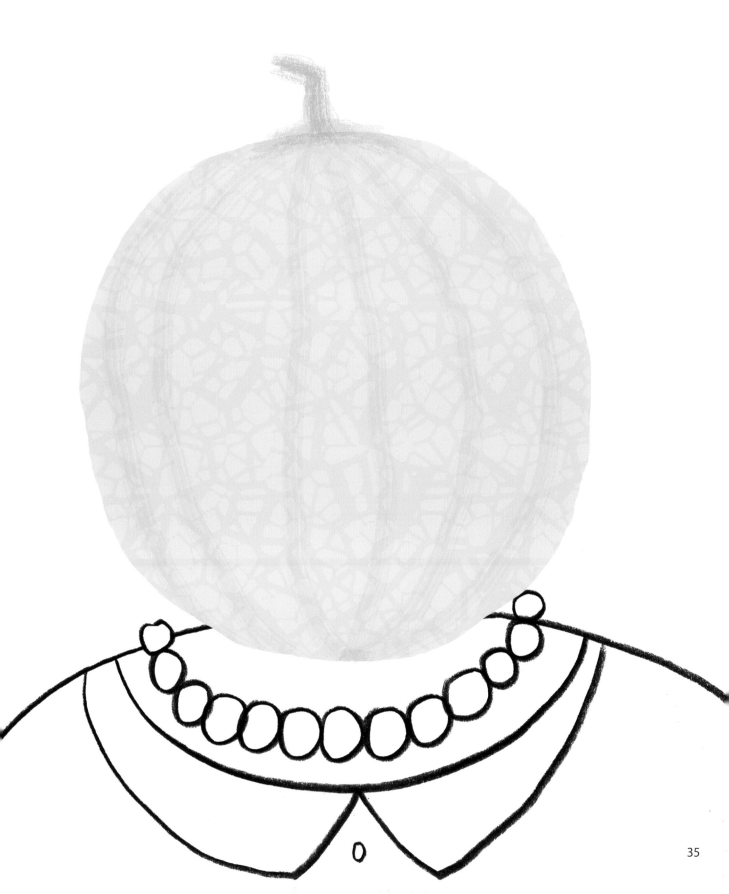

**Use the paper cutouts at the back of the book or your colored pencils to draw cakes, cupcakes, doughnuts . . . yummy!**

**Wash the dirty dishes using a white correction pen.**

**Then decorate the clean dishes with your pens or markers.**

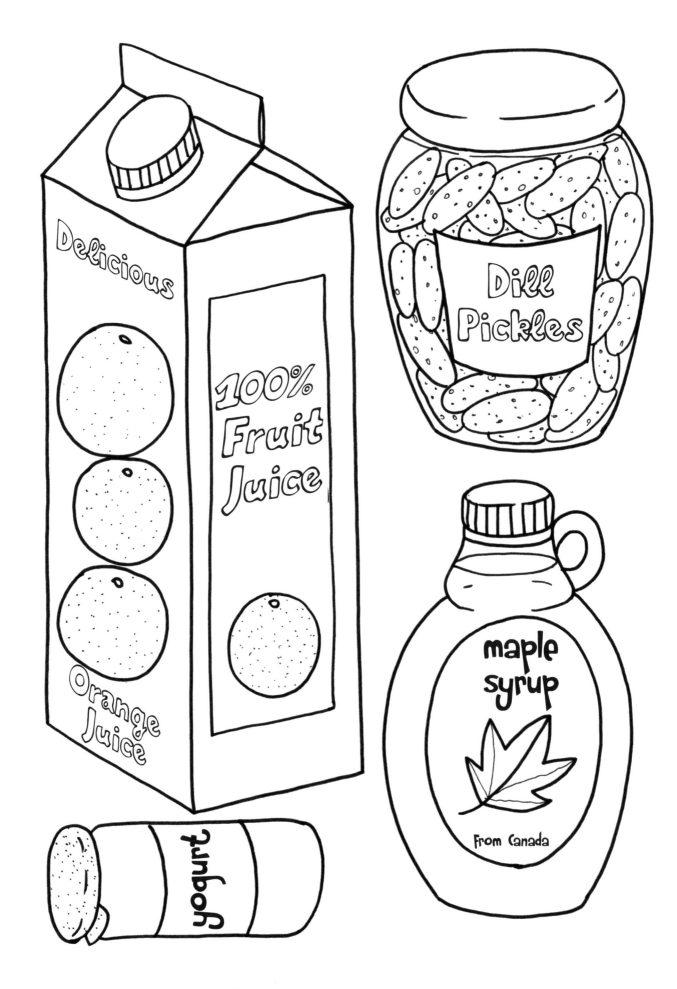

Delicious

100% Fruit Juice

Orange Juice

Dill Pickles

maple syrup

From Canada

yogurt

40

**Color all the packages.**

**Before serving the tea, decorate the cups and pot with different patterns.**

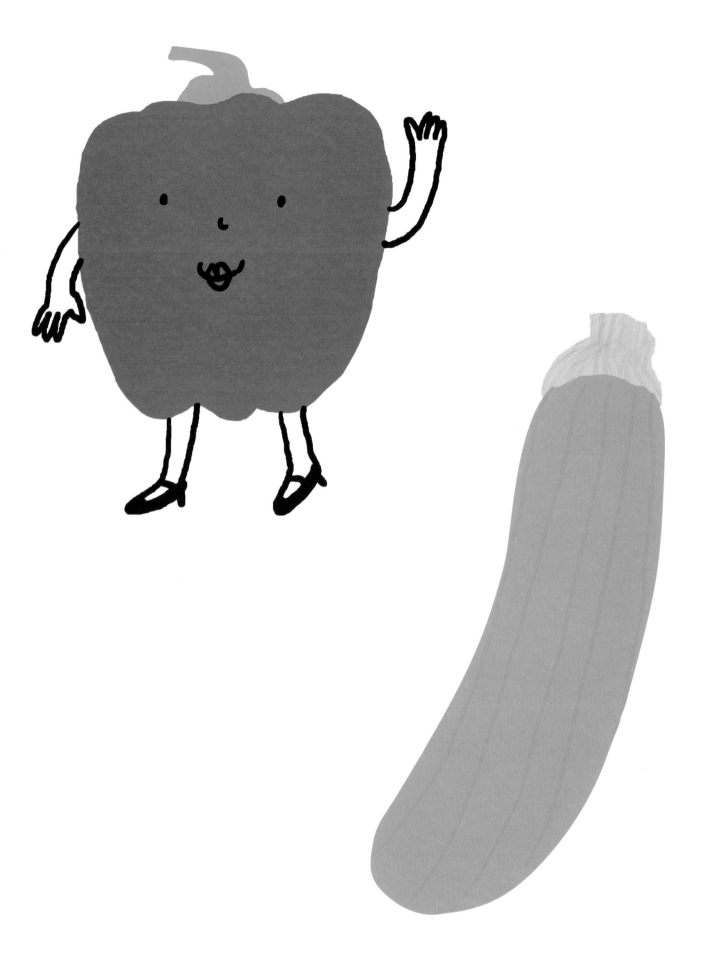

**Ms. Pepper says hello to her friends Mr. Cucumber and Ms. Eggplant. How will you decorate them?**

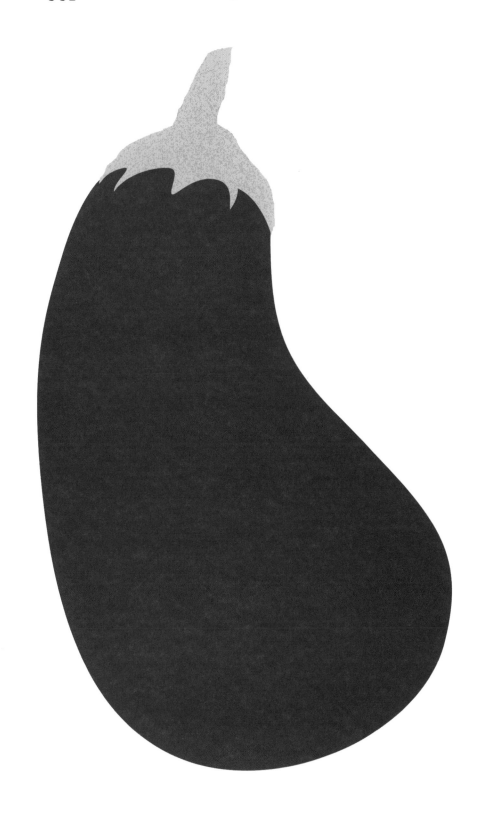

**What have these chefs done to their aprons? Color them and find out.**

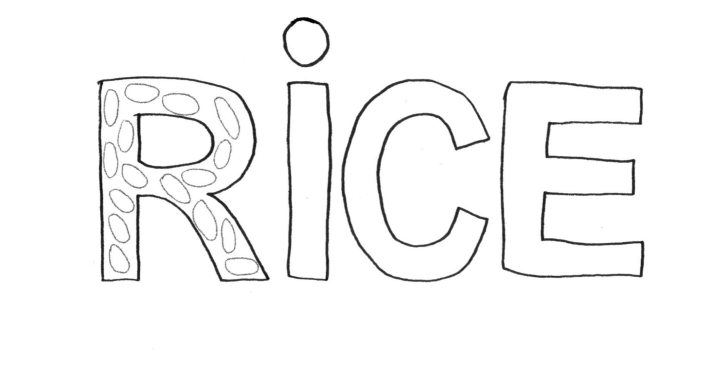

# RICE

# CAKES

# JAM

**Continue decorating each word.**

CHOCOLATE

PEAS

SUGAR

**Use your stickers to create three fruit pies.**

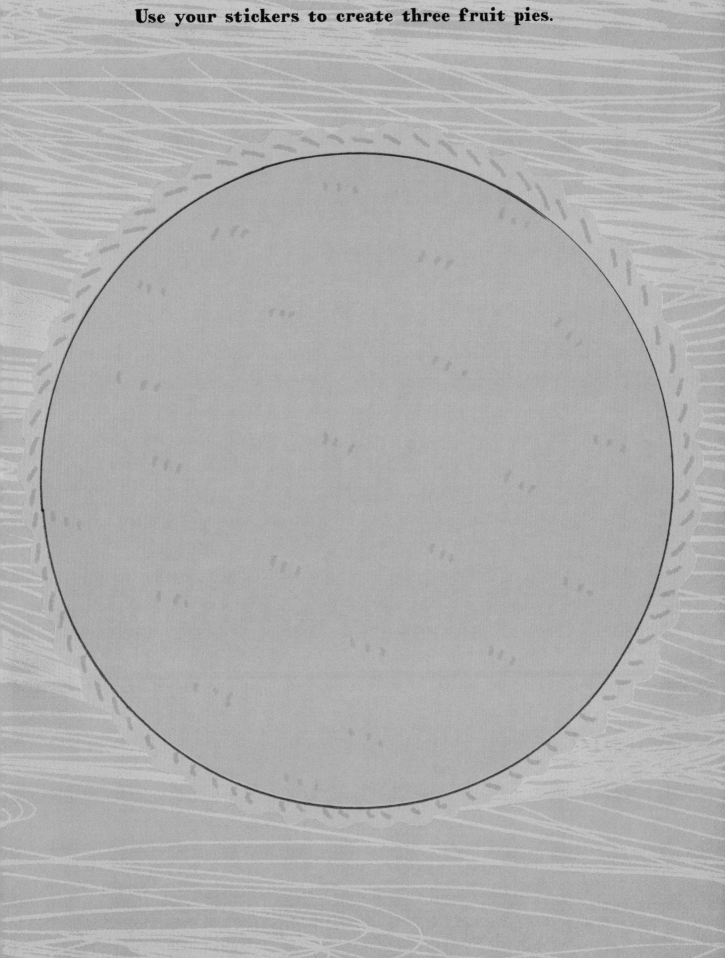

An empty refrigerator?
How sad. Fill it up!

54  **Use the paper cutouts at the back of the book to make two sandwiches.**

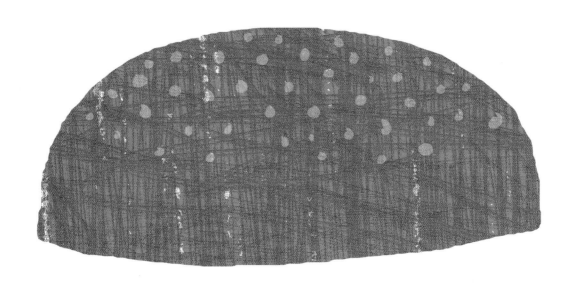

Mr. Hard-boiled Egg is
waiting for Mrs. Egg.
Draw her!

56

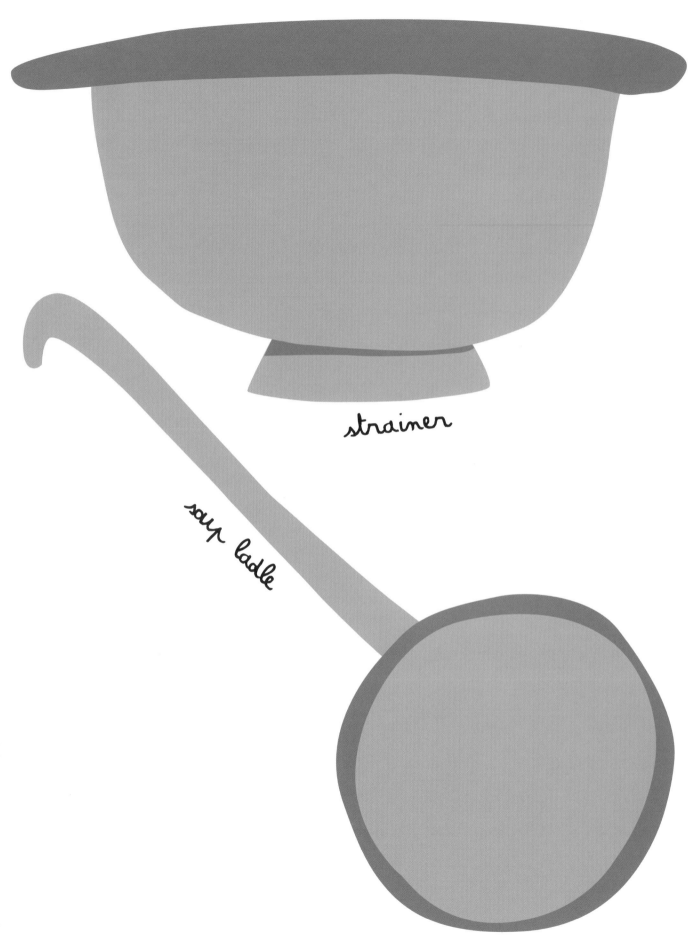

strainer

soup ladle

Use a black pen to draw the correct pattern on each utensil.

grater

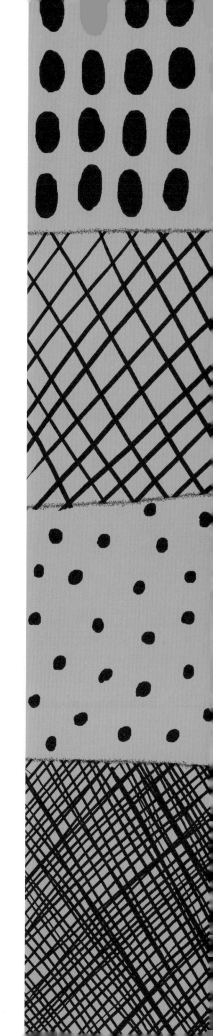

tea strainer

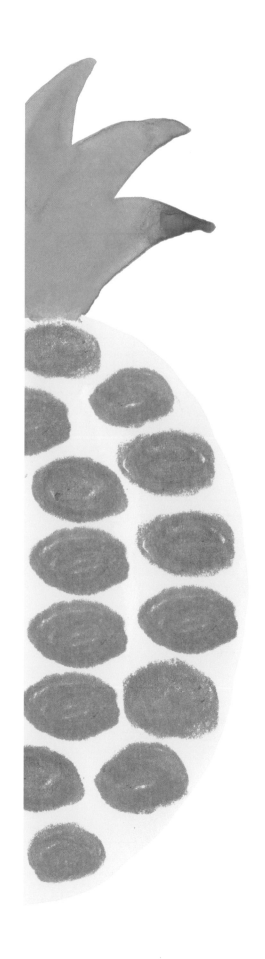

60 **Here are a pineapple, a pear, and an orange. Draw their other halves.**

On the plate, draw vegetables to go with the turkey.

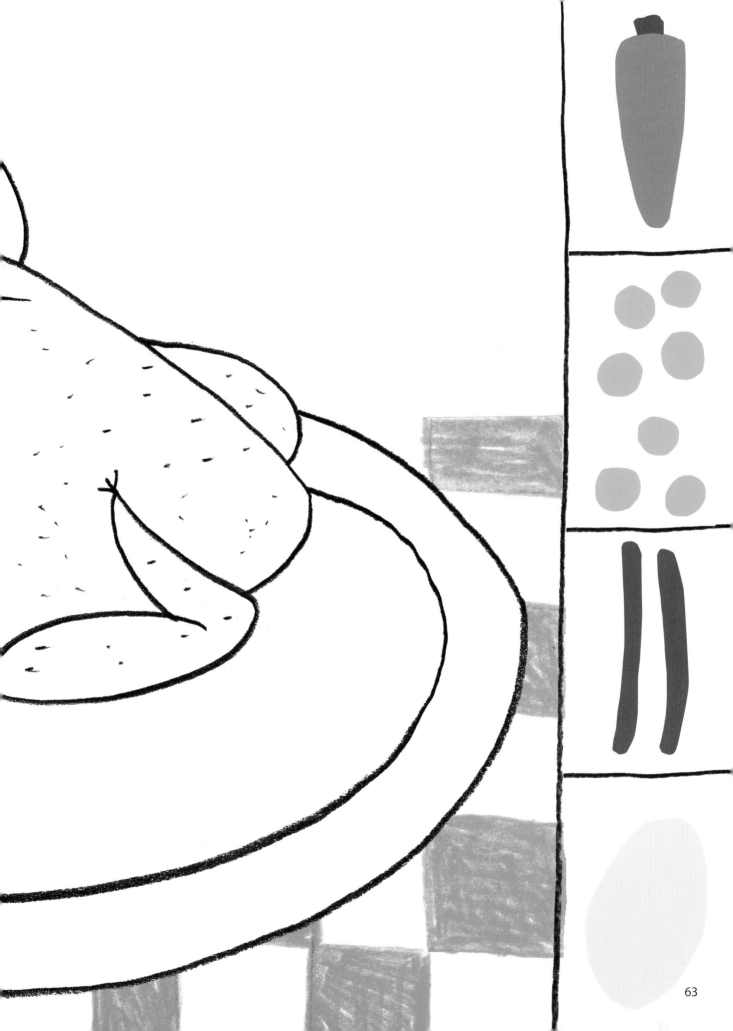

**Yum! Color the lollipops and then draw some more to fill up the bag of candy.**

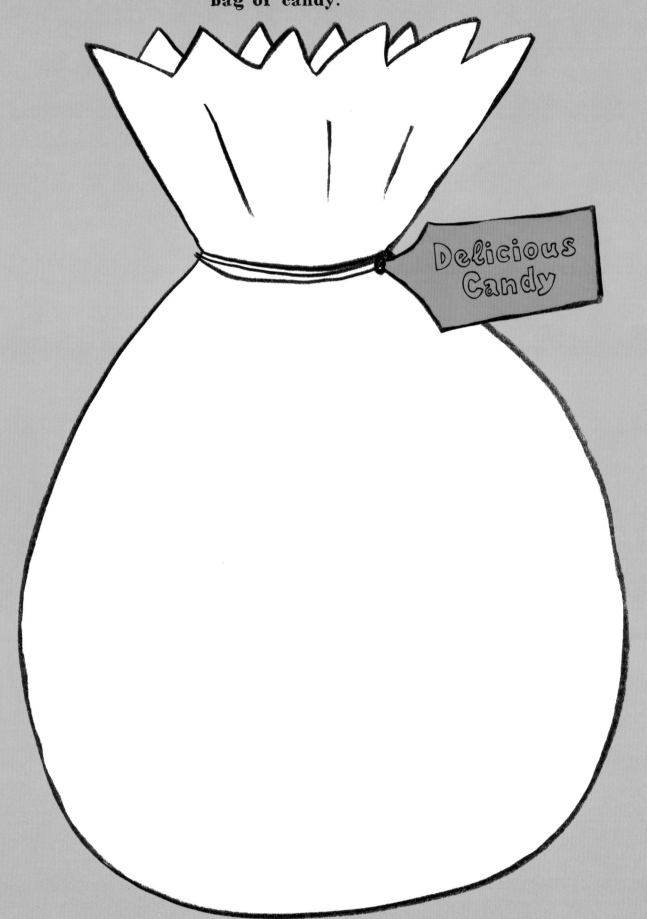

Delicious Candy

# Cake with raspberries

3 eggs
2/3 cup of sugar
3/4 cup of flour
1 packet of yeast
2/3 cup of butter
2/3 cup of fresh raspberries

Preheat the oven to 375°F. Beat eggs and sugar in a bowl. Add the flour, melted butter, and yeast while stirring gently. Add the raspberries. Pour into a buttered pan and bake for 50 minutes.

**To decorate this cookbook, draw the ingredients that go in the cake.**

**Using a marker, add the tomato sauce so the spaghetti isn't too bland.**

etti with

sauce

It's your birthday! Add sticker candles to your cake
and then draw yourself blowing them out.

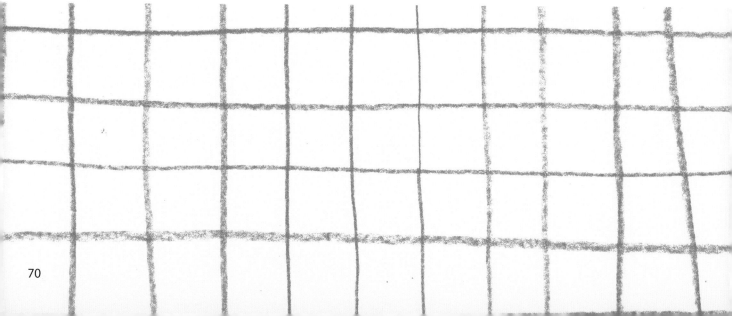

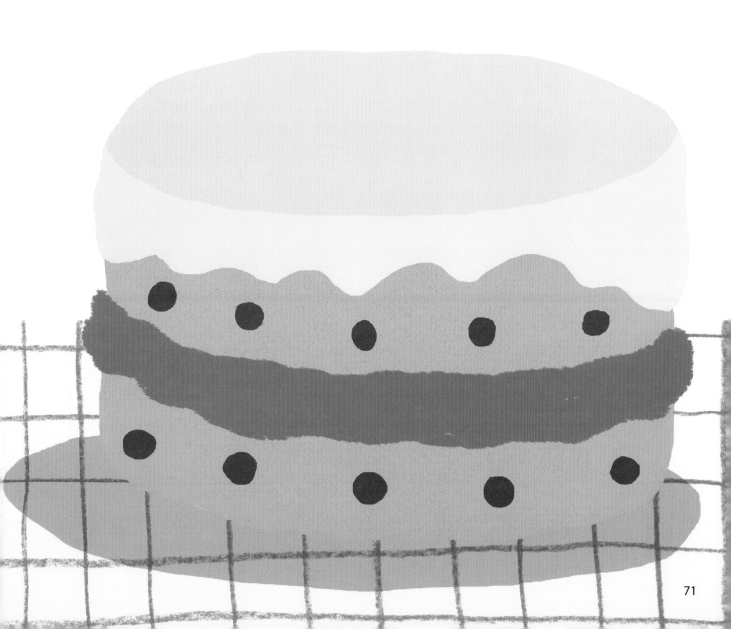

**You're the chef. Draw your self-portrait!**

Activity page 71

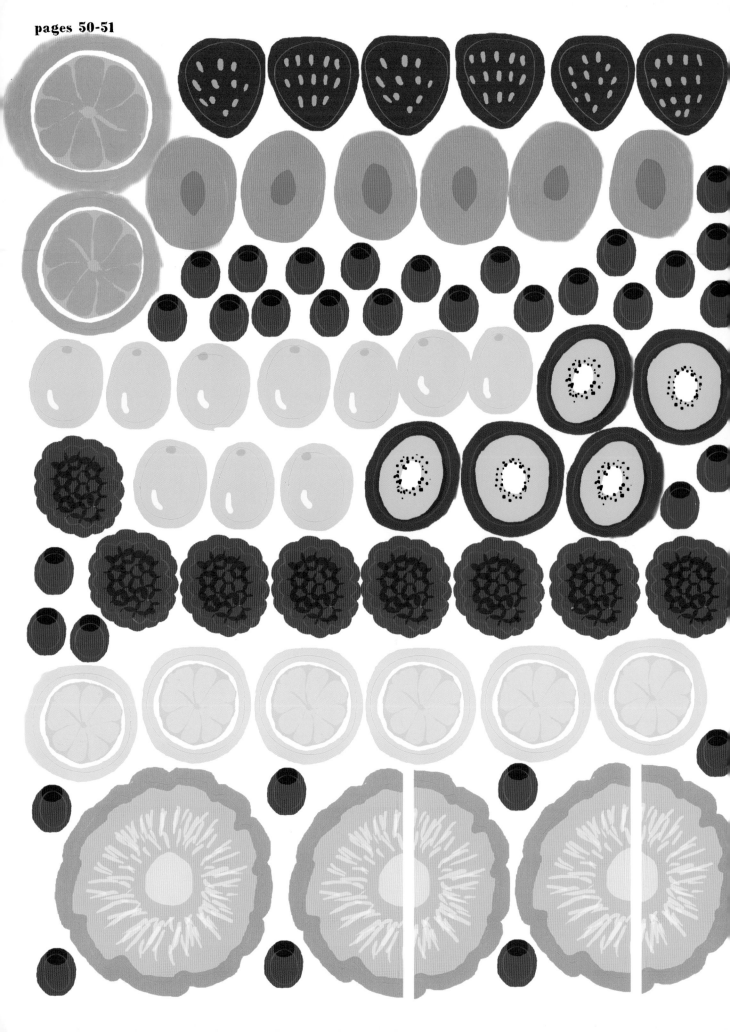

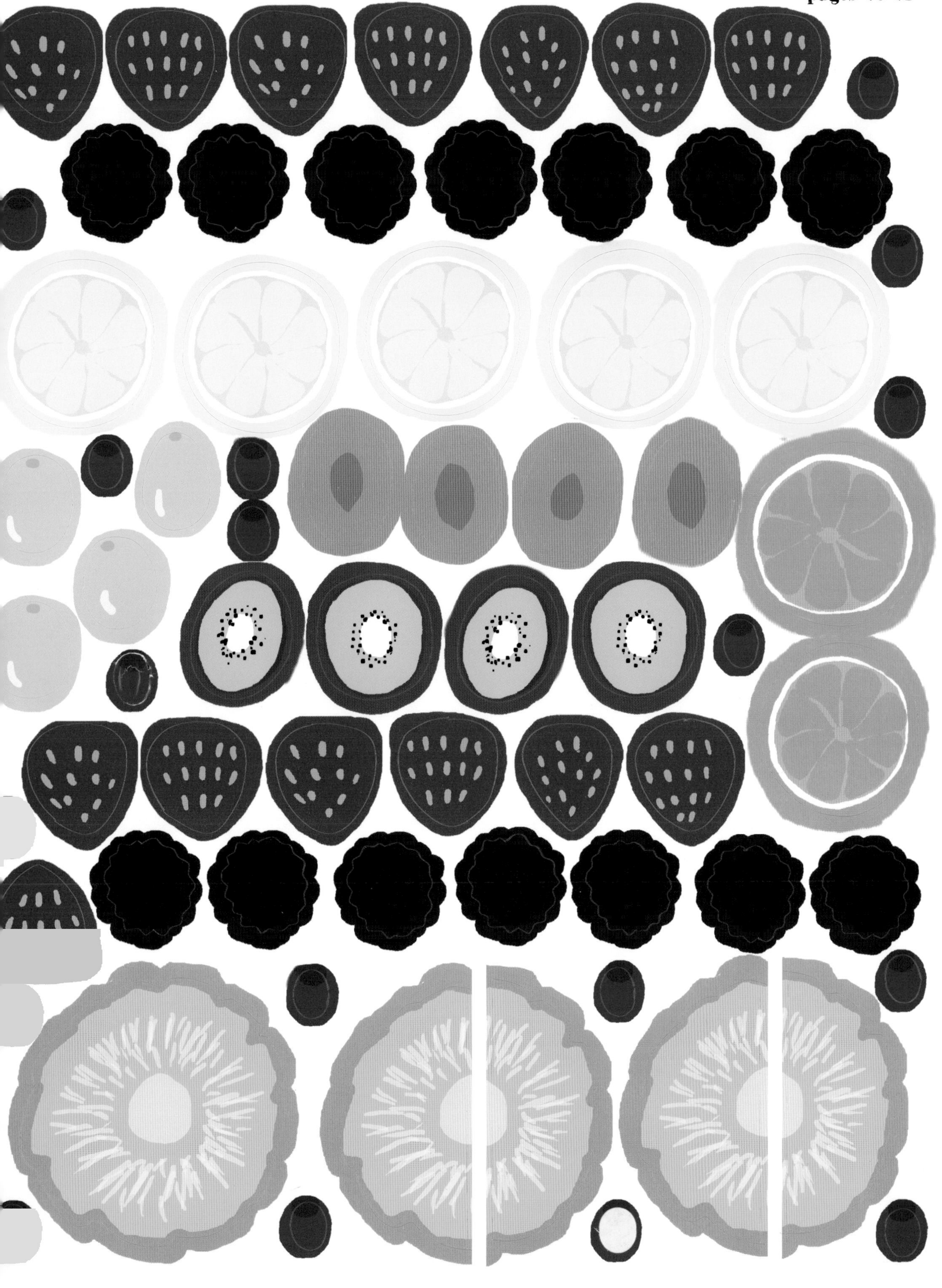

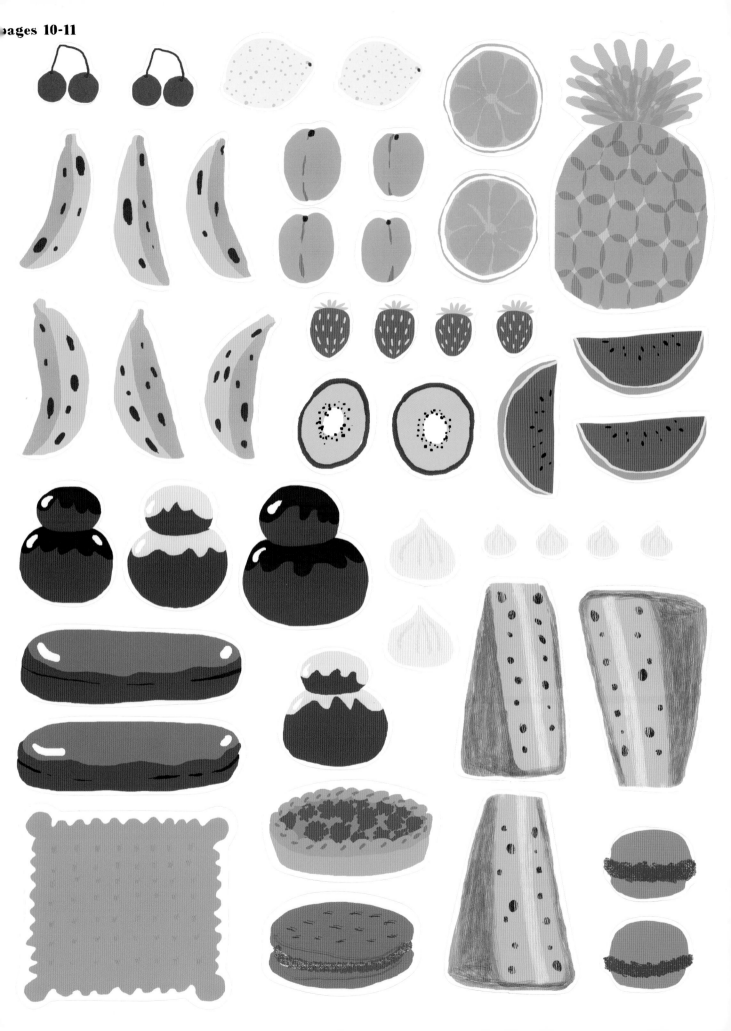

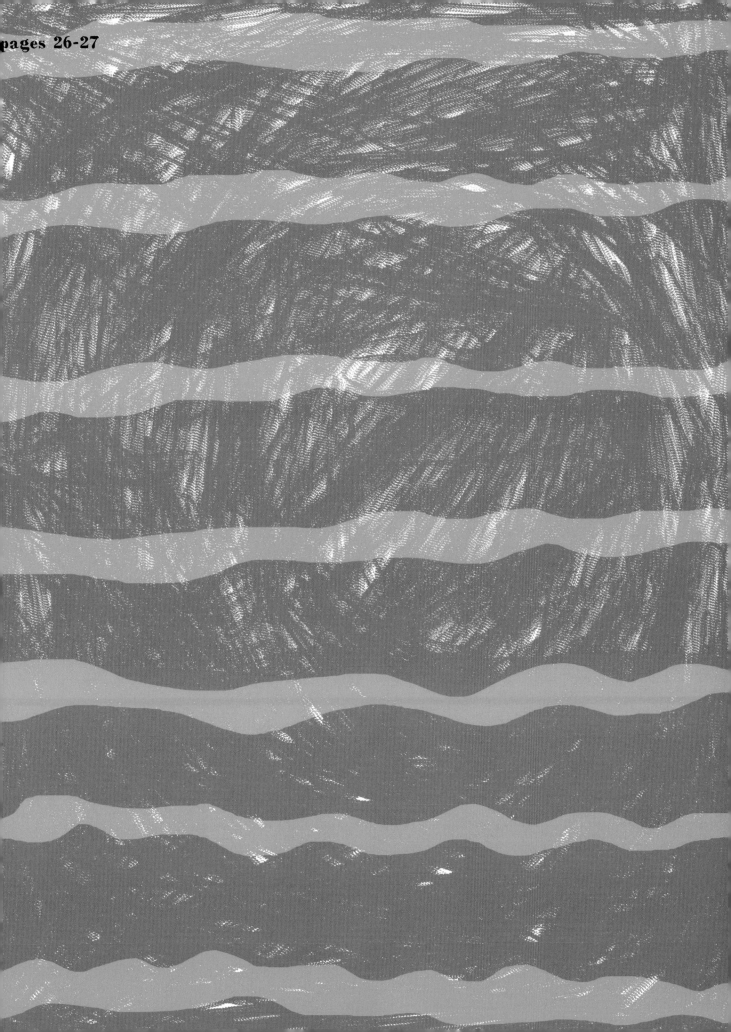

pages 26-27

pages 26-27

pages 26-27

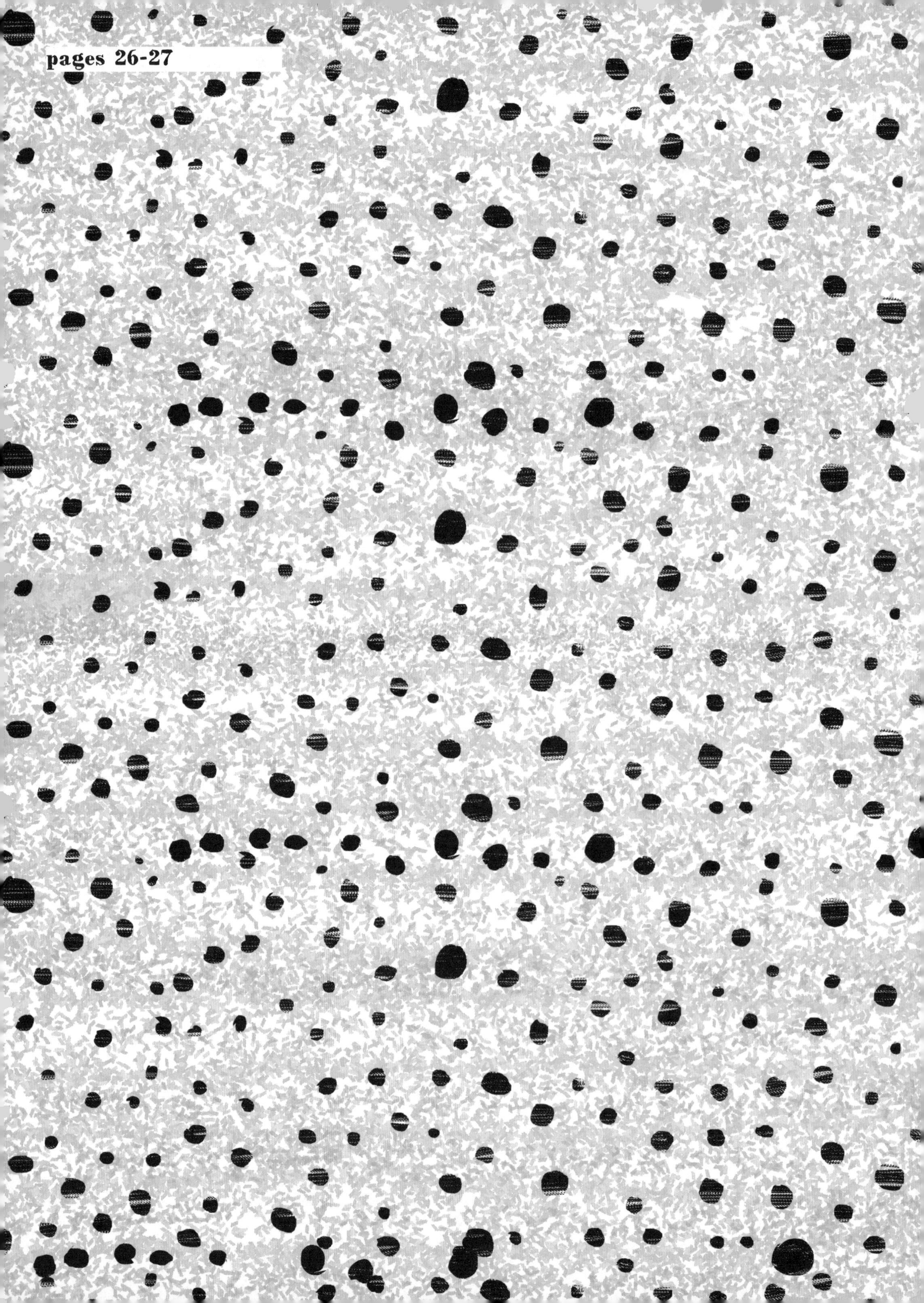

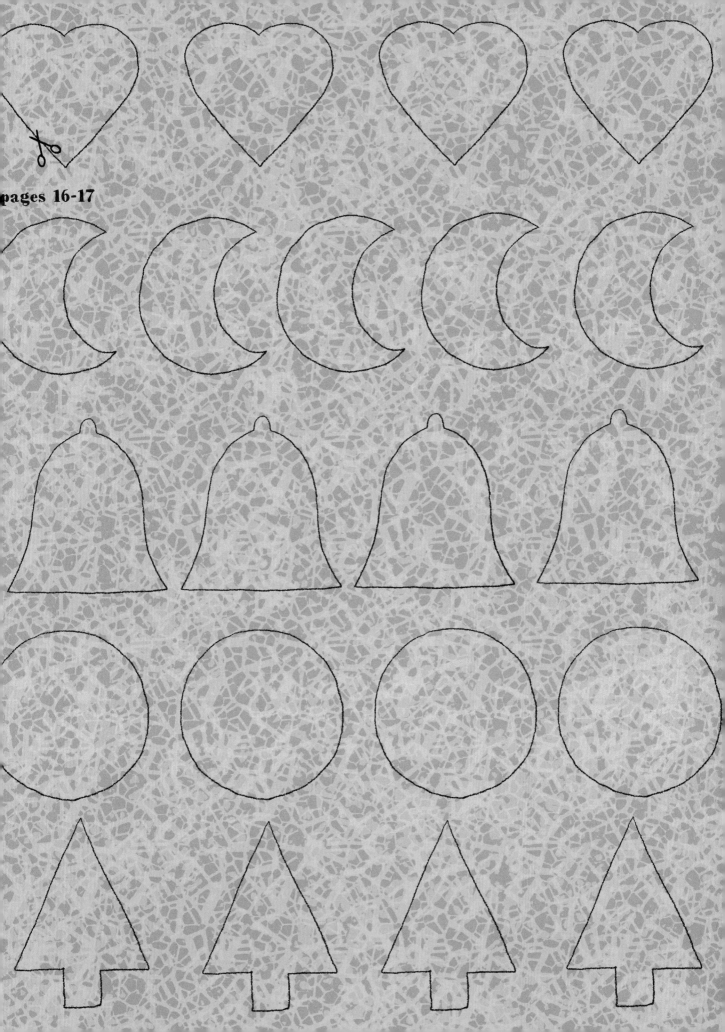

pages 16-17

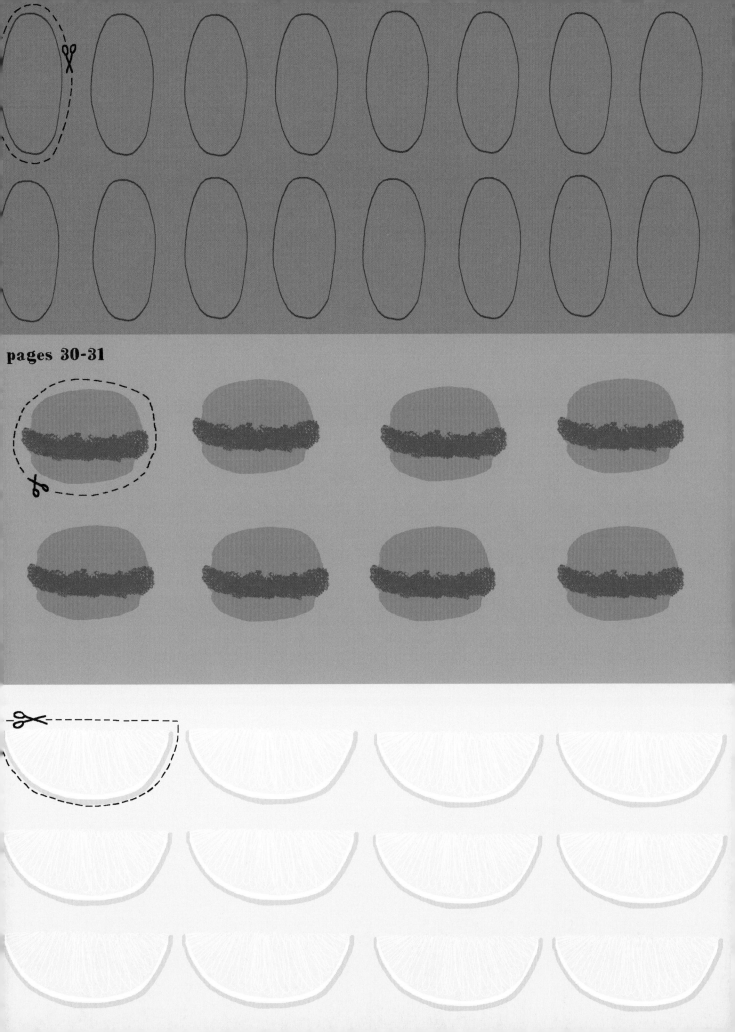

pages 30-31

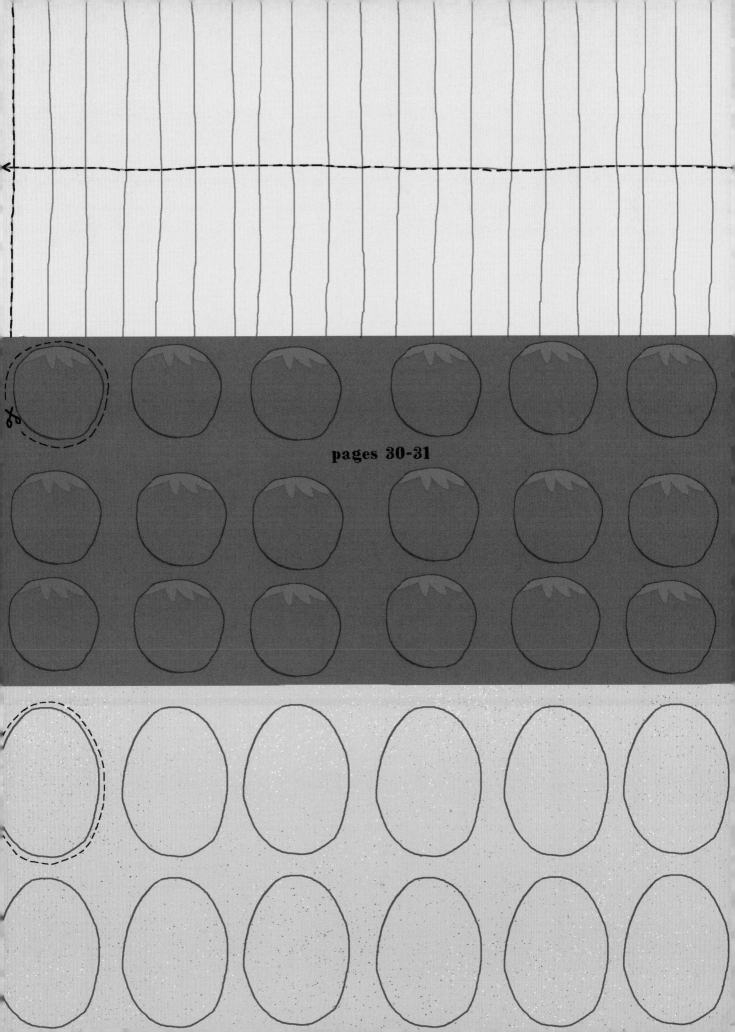

pages 30-31

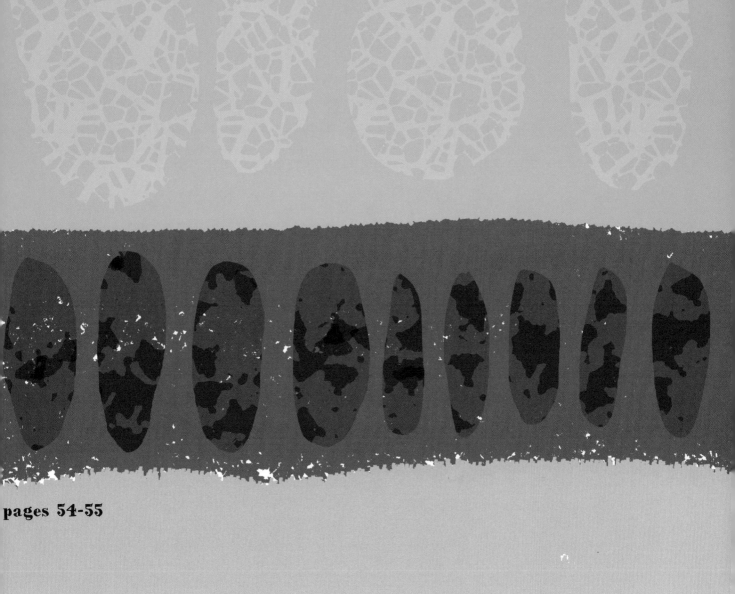

pages 54-55

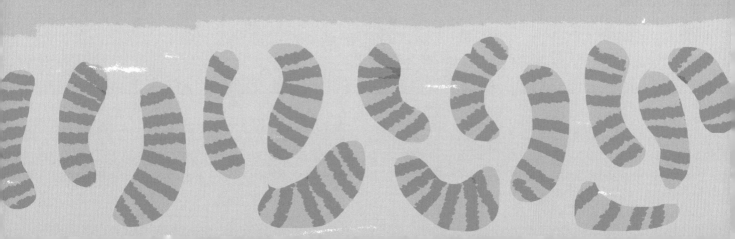

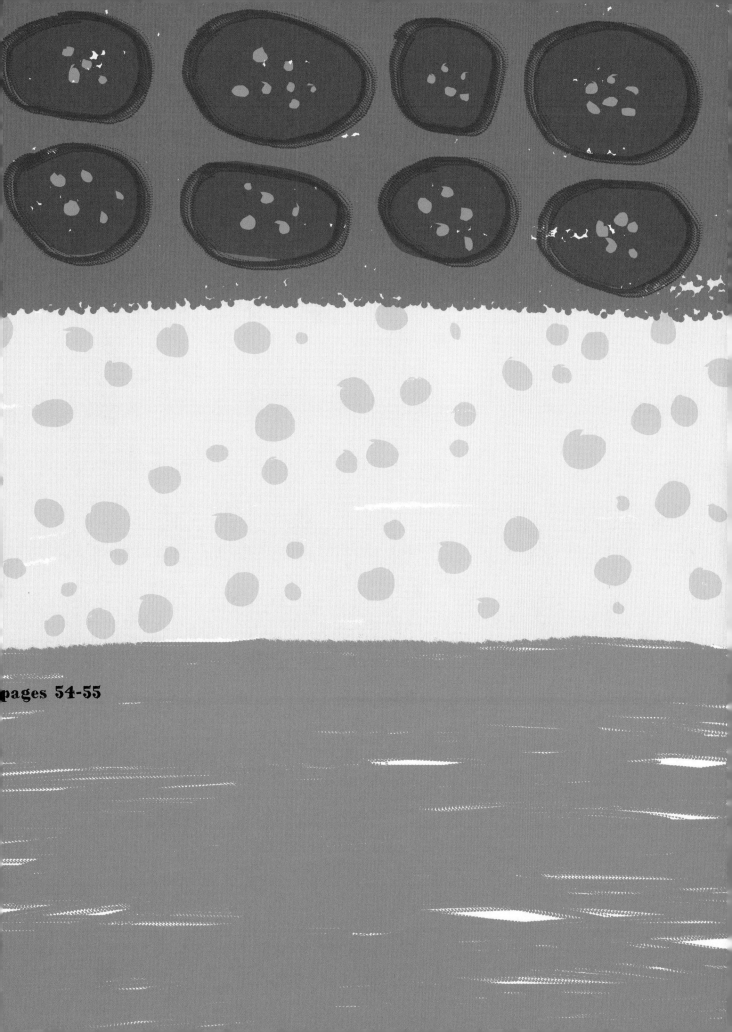

pages 54-55